Architecture must be a poetic expression of social justice.

Towards an Ethical Architecture

Issues within the Work of Gregory Henriquez

Alberto Pérez-Gómez

Christopher Grabowski

Helena Grdadolnik

Jim Green

May So

David Weir
EDITOR

BLUE*im*PRINT

Contents

Foreword

I AM AN ARCHITECT. As long as I can remember I have been immersed in the world of architecture. My father is an architect, a third generation architect. The firm of Henriques Brothers of Kingston, Jamaica evolved within our family mythology into Henriquez Partners of Vancouver, Canada. For a hundred years, our family has lived and breathed architecture. By the age of nineteen, I thought I knew what architecture was.

Then in 1982, I went to architecture school in Ottawa and met a thirty-four-year-old professor named Alberto Pérez-Gómez. He became the school's new director while I was in second year. I was one of many alienated youth who felt an absence of meaning, order and clarity in the experiences presented to us by the modern world. This man rocked our world. In the early 1980s, Carleton University's School of Architecture was a centre of architectural experimentation. Young professors came from Cranbrook, having studied with Daniel Libeskind; they came from Cooper Union having studied under John Hejduk. Aldo Rossi's first trip to North America was to Ottawa.

What did Alberto Pérez-Gómez teach us? He taught us about the history of architecture and how the profession has come to its current state of collective amnesia. Our new director created an environment where we were encouraged to learn from the past, to trust our embodied experience of the world, to explore our own stories and to find an authentic expression beyond style and conventional archetypes. The process from intention to drawing, drawing to model and model to the ultimate naming of the work was taught with rigour and devotion. I followed Alberto to McGill for graduate school, and there he introduced me to the ideas and work of Frederick Kiesler. Kiesler was the first architect I encountered who addressed the cosmic void—God's absence—in a way that resonated with my experience of the world. Why had nobody ever heard of Kiesler and his design of the Endless House? I was inspired by Kiesler's concept of endless space and the existential writings of Martin Buber. The intention was to explore the *hallowing of the everyday* within the rituals of daily life, with the goal of once again connecting the individual with the larger cosmic order.

I came back to Vancouver from Montreal and tried teaching at UBC School of Architecture, but I was 26 years old, still too young to command respect or have the patience to be of much use to my students. Then in 1989, inspired by my father's example, I threw my body, self and passion into his architectural practice. Richard Henriquez taught me how to build, make contracts and trust my hands. Together, we were going to make a difference.

I experimented with surrealist techniques in the design of my early buildings only to learn that the communities I was engaging with were made up of real people, who were not necessarily interested in such a personal project. Up until 1994, John Patkau was my mentor in the AIBC registration process and my father was the architect of record for the buildings I designed. Finally, I wrote the NCARB exams and became a registered architect and a partner with the firm Henriquez Partners. Shortly afterwards I met and was hired by Jim Green, then a provincial bureaucrat, and the newly formed Main and Hastings Housing Society to work on what would become Bruce Eriksen Place. Our office had been near the Downtown Eastside my whole childhood. I worked there most summers. Why did I know so little about the Downtown Eastside community? The answer was simple: I was a privileged Westside boy who had grown up in the comfort of the Jewish community.

My father had designed social housing early in his career, but why had he stopped? From his experience, he felt that the Canada Mortgage and Housing Corporation was less than pleased when one of his social housing projects, designed for Russian immigrants and completed below budget, turned out to be more attractive than the market housing surrounding it. It is not surprising that other design-oriented architects are not keen to engage in such a process. But the problem is more complex than this. Why are the best and brightest of my generation teaching, or designing new art galleries and obsessively detailed houses, while demonstrating no interest in the problems of marginalized people? If the humanist project is to once again unite humanity in the *chora*, the sacred cosmic dance, wouldn't the first step be to ensure that we all have a roof over our heads, food in our bellies and support structures in our lives that enable participation?

Working with these new clients from the Downtown Eastside, it quickly became apparent to me that their desires went beyond mere shelter. Excluded from partaking in the material excesses of middle-class North American life, they struggled with issues of orientation, community, and ultimately, the meaning of life – the same concerns being confronted in contemporary theoretical architectural discourse. These were the clients I yearned for; at the very least, we would build beautiful housing and at best, we might help make a meaningful difference in people's lives.

The integration of the poetic and the ethical became my new project. I spent the following ten years experimenting, attempting in each project to balance social content and the search for symbols providing collective orientation. I came to realize that my role as an architect was not merely as a consultant for hire, but as an individual whose values and beliefs demanded action. The serious social, political and environmental climate since 9/11 required many of us to more carefully examine the reality of the forces shaping our economic world order. From this new perspective, the larger questions now seem clear. Who am I serving? Who do I represent? What type of work will I do? These are not questions of ability, but of ethics.

GREGORY HENRIQUEZ

Vancouver • June 2006

Introduction

AT FORTY-THREE, Gregory Henriquez is still considered young in the world of architecture. He has a long and promising career ahead of him, so why the need for a book on his work now? For one, Henriquez is embarking on the most challenging project of his career, the Woodward's Redevelopment. This is a momentous and highly anticipated project in the city of Vancouver, and one that may guide the direction of Henriquez Partners Architects for years to come. But this book does not merely present the architect and his work; instead, they are used as a springboard to a larger discussion concerning the role of the architect in today's society. Gregory Henriquez is part of a new generation proclaiming the danger of architects becoming instruments of private interest, consultants for hire whose authority has fallen into doubt.

Alberto Pérez-Gómez wrote in *The Architect's Metier*: "Our situation in history seems to demand a profound questioning of the commonly held assumptions and beliefs of our society ... Can we simply accept that our role as individuals is to produce consumption goods and services for a hedonistic society? Can we believe that the value of our lives as professionals can be measured by our economic success?" He goes on to say, "The role of the architect in society is unclear. From a total corruption and misunderstanding of his role in the form of planner, project manager and businessman, to the well-intentioned but often misguided production of images, the value of his contributions is highly suspect."

While few would deny that architecture involves compromise and that the client's desires often take precedent, it is a true architect who understands the inextricable obligation to the public interest regardless of who is paying the bills. As May So points out in her examination of the Woodward's Redevelopment at the book's conclusion, the ethical dimension of architectural practice is not a new or optional role, but an integral part of practice as described in the Architect's Oath administered by each provincial association as part of the registration process. Every architect in Canada has sworn, "I promise now that my professional conduct as it concerns the community, my work, and my fellow architects will be governed by the ethics and tradition of this honourable and learned profession." [1] In exchange for bearing such a weighty responsibility, the architectural profession enjoys the right to engage in self-regulation. This means that change can and must come from within.

When working primarily with the client's interest in mind, the architect's role is relegated to service-provider and the product reflects nothing more than the client's desires. David Childs of the architecture firm SOM described this attitude within his own work aptly when he confided, "I know a lot of what I've designed is not 'A' work, but my role was different. I wanted to raise the level of everyday development as much as I could."[2] But is this enough, should architects not have a simultaneous obligation to their clients, to themselves and to society?

Some architects work with a strong personal vision that becomes the driving rationale for a project's aesthetic. Developers and public institutions have started engaging "celebrity" or "star" architects to increase a project's value, ease it through tricky political territory, create fundraising opportunities, raise sale prices and promote cultural tourism. Architecture in this case is depicted as an agent of commercial interests. Popular media sources present such signature buildings and their celebrity architects as fashion commodities. Why should we be surprised, then, that the public has lost faith in the architect's ability to represent the public good? In The New York Times, Nicolai Ouroussoff spoke of this problem, singling out Frank Gehry particularly from the other star architects: "Few would question Mr. Gehry's talent. The question is whether he has allowed his experimental ethos to be harnessed for the sake of maximizing a developer's profits. It is also fair to ask whether Mr. Gehry and other gifted architects have made a pact with the Devil, compromising their values for the sake of ever bigger commissions." He continues later in the article, "Not so long ago American architects complained that they were shut out of the public dialogue. Today they work in a climate in which building is booming, and architecture is revered, but as an aesthetic, not a social, force."[3]

The crux of Alberto Pérez-Gómez's essay included in this book is that neither the ethical nor the aesthetic alone is enough; the two must work in combination to produce architecture that is meaningful to society. In the essay he connects the personal creative force of the architect and the inherently public medium of architecture as follows: although it is important for architects to ask pertinent ethical questions and to use their imagination to form architecture, they do not control its ultimate meaning; society does. According to Pérez-Gómez we live in a time and space that lacks meaningful collective rituals, where

1 Each member upon notice of registration shall make and subscribe to the following declaration:
Solemnly do I declare that having read and understood the Act of the Architectural Institute of British Columbia, its Bylaws and Code of Conduct, and having passed the examinations, I am eligible for membership. Further do I announce that I will uphold professional aims, and the art, and the science, of architecture and thereby improve the environment. I also accept with obligation the need to further my education as an architect. I promise now that my professional conduct as it concerns the community, my work, and my fellow architects will be governed by the ethics and the tradition of this honourable and learned profession.

individual greed has infiltrated the core of our world's ordering principles. Architects have the power to aid in the collective orientation of our communities, rather than act as mere decorators who camouflage the void. To Pérez-Gómez, architecture needs to be a poetic expression of social justice. This theory became one of two positions upon which Henriquez has built his practice; community activism and advocacy represented by Jim Green make up the other half.

My interview with Jim Green was conceived as a counterpoint to the text by Alberto Pérez-Gómez, but upon further inspection more parallels exist between the academic stance of Pérez-Gómez and Jim Green, the activist, than one might initially presume. Quoting Herbert Muschamp, former architecture critic at The New York Times, Jim Green asserts that a community's collective memory can convey meaning on a building like Woodward's and that its status is not necessarily a product of its design. Pérez-Gómez uses the destruction of the World Trade Center towers to make a similar point: once a work of architecture enters the public realm its meaning lies beyond the architect's control and may differ from the author's intent.

In the conversation, Jim Green makes clear his belief that a dialectical engagement between the architect and the community will result in meaningful architecture. It is not enough to provide housing for those in need, according to Green, but the disenfranchised must be empowered by being involved early in the design process, and the aesthetic dimension cannot be an afterthought.

Beauty cannot be stripped away from ethical design. The Functionalists of the Modern movement tried to do so when creating large works built for the social good. Pruitt-Igoe particularly comes to mind. When the social housing mega-project opened in 1956 its spartan forms were fêted by the architectural press with typical sterile photos of the buildings untainted by people and the ephemera of everyday life. Less than two decades later Pruitt-Igoe was deemed uninhabitable—even downright dangerous. It was demolished in a public display on March 16, 1972. The lesson from Pruitt-Igoe is that it isn't enough for architects to design buildings that cover the basic needs of people; the architect also has to engage the community.

2 **Nicolai Ouroussoff**, *The Power Broker Yearns to be Cool*. THE NEW YORK TIMES, February 20, 2005.

3 **Nicolai Ouroussoff**, *Skyline for Sale*. THE NEW YORK TIMES, June 4, 2006.

Samuel Mockbee, the founder of Rural Studio, stated well architecture's potential contribution to society: *"Architecture more than any other art form is a social art, and for those of us who design and build, we must do so with an awareness of a more socially and physically responsive architecture. The architect's primary emotional connection should always be with place, and not just the superficial qualities of place, but the ethical responsibility of shaping the environment, of breaking up social complacency and energizing one's community."* [4]

Henriquez Partners tries to create architecture that shapes its environment and energizes a community. Christopher Grabowski's photojournalism investigates a selection of their buildings to explore the space between the architecture and its inhabitants. Grabowski's photographs remind us that architecture plays a meaningful role in the fabric of our daily lives. Alongside the images, a story emerges from May So's texts accompanying the ten projects; it traces Gregory Henriquez's history from architectural student at Carleton University to his partnership with his father Richard Henriquez and Ivo Taller; it shows his evolution from academic studies to a practicing architect conflicted by the need to find a way to engage with the community.

The book closes with the promise of Woodward's, a project that is bringing Gregory Henriquez closer to his ultimate goal of seamlessly integrating aesthetics and ethics. Architectural theory and architectural practice were separated in the early nineteenth century and have since become almost isolated endeavours. Gregory Henriquez has been attempting to reestablish a common ground between them by forging a synthesis of theoretical explorations, community activism and the present realities of architectural practice in North America.

HELENA GRDADOLNIK

Vancouver • June 2006

---

4 **Samuel Mockbee**, *The Role of the Citizen Architect.* GOOD DEEDS, GOOD DESIGN: COMMUNITY SERVICE THROUGH ARCHITECTURE. Ed. Brian Bell. New York: Princeton Architectural Press, 2004. 156.

Firehall Training Tower · COQUITLAM, BC 1985

FOLLOWING INITIAL ASSAULTS on the Modern Movement and a retreat into historicism, the architectural climate in the early 1980s was characterized by a search for a generative theory of architecture. Theorists such as Peter Eisenmen and Daniel Libeskind proclaimed the end of meaningful architectural practice. They advanced a practice of critical commentary through architectural explorations confined to drawing, models and words, with the objective of revealing the absence of collective meaning. In response, theorists like Alberto Pérez-Gómez and Juhani Pallasmaa promoted the built representation of perceptual experience, identifying the body as a locus for disclosing meaning within the world. In the context of these theoretical debates Gregory Henriquez undertook his architectural training at Carleton University, where Pérez-Gómez was director from 1983 to 1986.

The Firehall Training Tower, designed by Gregory at Henriquez & Partners in the summer after his third year at Carleton, is situated in the back training yard of the Coquitlam Firehall, the first project of a new town centre for the rapidly growing Vancouver suburb of Coquitlam. In developing the overall plan for this placeless, undeveloped suburban landscape, Richard Henriquez aimed to give the town centre an identity and rationalize the orientation of programmatic elements on the site by creating a fictional history of renovation and growth. The first phase of fictional growth dispersed "original" small-town commercial brick buildings on the site to form the "historic" nucleus of the development. Then "new" concrete block elements were used to transform and displace the nucleus, generating the firehall's final configuration.

The intent of the training tower's design was to make a critical commentary on the groundless instability of modern life in the suburban landscape. An abstracted concrete block suburban house was severed. Half was displaced to the top of the canted steel frame tower, whose architectural language was inspired by the Soviet Constructivists' largely unrealized ideas for communication towers, designed for the dissemination of propaganda. The severed suburban house rises above Coquitlam's sprawl to speak about the lack of authenticity that characterizes current North American development.

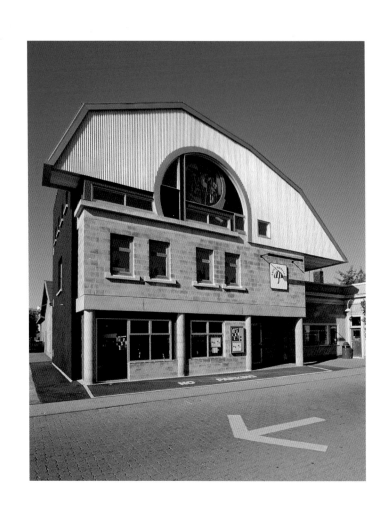

Arts Umbrella, Granville Island · VANCOUVER, BC 1987 & 1998

IN HIS FOURTH YEAR at Carleton University's School of Architecture, Gregory took part in a study abroad program in Kyoto, under Katsuhiko Muramoto. Deeply influenced by the Japanese view of the urban environment as pluralistic and fragmented, Gregory came to realize that the Western approach to urban development expressed in Cartesian geometry and zoning hierarchies is merely one system among many. Much of human experience—the mysterious, the fragmentary, the quest for orientation and meaning—is left unacknowledged by rational planning and building processes which define, restrict and separate human activities.

Gregory's first design project after graduation was an addition to Arts Umbrella, a non-profit arts institute for youth founded in 1979 by his mother Carol Henriquez, and Gloria Schwartz. Over 40,000 children a year now participate in the centre's various arts programs. Once an industrial peninsula, Granville Island's sheds, through a federal government initiative, were preserved and redeveloped in the early 1980s as a public waterfront destination. A transformation rather than a replica, the addition's design is a critical comment on the themed nature of Granville Island's industrial image.

Part of the addition's form was inspired by an adjacent one-storey stucco shed. Surreal juxta-positions, dislocations and scalar shifts, operations derived from the work of Surrealist architect Frederick Kiesler, were applied to transform the basic form. The resulting new front façade represents a fragmented oversized face. A large, leaded-glass window "eye" on the second floor looks down onto the street underneath the protective arch of a corrugated metal "cosmic eyebrow" roof. With windows at a child's eye level, the new studio spaces evoke the non-scalar imagination of a child.

Seeking a critique of the Arts Umbrella addition, Gregory wrote to Bruno Zevi, the editor of Italian magazine L'Architettura and an architect influenced by Frank Lloyd Wright's concept of organic architecture. Zevi responded in a letter dated January 26, 1991: "Yes, dear Gregory Henriquez, I want to publish your building—but the next one, not this one. Because this one is almost boxy, almost symmetrical, almost static in its spaces. Almost, but not quite. It is not academical, it is not Post-Modern. But certainly it is not modern. There is some courage in it, but it came after and not at the source."

For Arts Umbrella's next addition, Gregory demolished the original stucco shed and replaced it with a second transformation, this one more rectilinear than the first. The playful harmony and contrast between the first organic design and the second rectilinear addition represents the dialogue between the rational and subconscious impetuses behind the act of creation.

False Creek Community Centre, Granville Island • VANCOUVER, BC 1991 & 2001

ON RETURNING TO VANCOUVER from graduate school in 1989, Gregory approached Sandy Hirshen, then the director of the University of British Columbia's School of Architecture, with the idea of teaching a graduate level experimental studio in the Downtown Eastside. Gregory invited a group of six young architects, including Russell Acton, Mark Ostry and Bill Pechet, to direct the students in a broad exploration of space through the interpretive lens of the students' personal stories. Inspired by thoughts of future collaboration, the young architects established the Beef Levor Non-Profit Art Society—a derivative of a misprinted beef *liver* menu item—to promote and explore the art of architecture. While the Society was short-lived, it marked the beginning of Gregory's ongoing concern to position his architectural practice in the larger work of community engagement.

Adjacent to the Arts Umbrella addition, the original False Creek Community Centre was housed in an industrial shed renovated twenty years earlier as part of the original Granville Island redevelopment. The 1991 expansion preserved fragments of three adjacent severely deteriorating structures, suggesting their previous existence without attempting to lock them in the past. Out of this fragmentation, a new whole was achieved by superimposing two lines of force over the disparate buildings. The lines graphically trace circulation routes, slice and join various parts of the four buildings, and intersect at the lobby where they form the reception desk and become patterns on the floor.

In the second phase, built in 1999, a derelict boat shed that bordered the main access from the north was demolished to become the site of a new small-scale gymnasium, and an expanded fitness centre was inserted above the existing administration offices. Inspired by the spread wings of Granville Island's seagulls in flight, the gymnasium's roof trusses were constructed from single slabs of Timberstrand board with the negative shapes milled out to make an economic yet highly poetic structure. The milled-out shapes, typically discarded in the manufacturing process, were used to form benches in the expanded lobby.

The west courtyard, designed in the first phase of expansion to mediate the space between the community centre and a children's water park, was given the shape of a woman's breast in plan. The design inspiration is not readily apparent to those using the courtyard. As Gregory's humanist approach matures, his projects are exploring increasingly direct translations of bodily forms into architecture.

Bella Bella Community School · WAGLISLA, CAMPBELL ISLAND, BC 1993

BELLA BELLA COMMUNITY SCHOOL was Gregory's first foray into the difficult ethical terrain of community development projects, the mainstay of his present work. The Heiltsuk people living on the Bella Bella Band Reserve on British Columbia's central coast are beset by challenges common to many First Nations communities in Canada. Unemployment, industrialization of fishing and education of children in church-run residential schools until the mid 1970s have eroded cultural traditions and language. In working with the Heiltsuk people, Gregory had to consider the extent to which architecture is able to address a community's needs and desires.

The Heiltsuk, who now number thirteen hundred compared to many thousands before European contact, are working to reconstruct their culture. An article by Stephen Hume in The Vancouver Sun on December 6, 1991 attributed the steady recovery of the Heiltsuk to former elected chief councillor Cecil Reid's progressive and controversial leadership. He replaced utilitarian public housing with distinctive homes symbolizing community pride and self-determination. Wanting to expand the community school, Reid empowered the School Board, made up primarily of mothers, to commission Henriquez & Partners. The new addition, which links the separate elementary and secondary school buildings, consists of classrooms, kindergartens, a gymnasium, office space and a room where elders teach the Heiltsuk language.

Inspired by the community's struggles to reclaim their traditional heritage, Gregory infused the program with ritual and mythological symbolism drawn from Heiltsuk history. The entry and circulation spine of the new school became the body of the creator, a raven, emerging from the side of a long house and clutching a giant crystal. After the School Board accepted the design, Ed Newman, the traditional hereditary chief, became the elected chief. Newman and the elders reproached the School Board for neglecting to include them in the decision-making process and would not sanction the use of the raven as a cultural symbol.

The elders appointed David Gladstone, a local Heiltsuk artist, to rewrite the mythological program in collaboration with the project team. While accepting a Western school typology, Gladstone envisioned a new ground for it, inspired by the Heiltsuk's traditional concept of nature as classroom. Gladstone revised the symbolism of the building to that of an eagle after being granted special permission by the Eagle Clan, one of the more influential Heiltsuk clans. Gladstone also modified the proportions on the front of the fragmented longhouse to more closely resemble a traditional longhouse.

Reflecting on his experience as Bella Bella's architect, Gregory noted, "Questions arising from these recent discussions revolve around the issues of identity and appropriation. In our architectural practice we encounter many different cultures, community groups and individuals. Our role as consultants is to, on one level, simply provide design services to our clients, yet we also feel a moral obligation to participate in these important discussions to help provide resolution." Gregory's experience with Bella Bella taught him the importance of working with a community's unique cultural identity, skills that would inform his architectural approach to future projects.

Ethics and Poetics in Architecture

CONTRARY TO COMMON ASSUMPTIONS, the discipline of architecture is very complex, shifting with history and culture and also remaining the same. In some ways it is analogous to the human condition, which demands that we continually address the same basic questions to come to terms with mortality and the possibility of cultural transcendence, while expecting diverse answers that are appropriate to specific times and places. Architecture, like other forms of making traditionally associated with the fine arts, is an ontological mutant. It has shifted throughout history and cannot be reduced to a species of works. It is a naïve prejudice to identify the tradition of architecture with a chronology of useful buildings whose main significance is to delight through aesthetic contemplation. This popular modern concept was a product of the Enlightenment and only came to fruition in the nineteenth century, particularly after the dissemination of J.N.L. Durand's *Recueil et Parallèle des Edifices de Tout Genre, Anciens et Modernes*, where architectural history is first presented as a progressive sequence of rational building types. A more careful appraisal of architectural traditions in diverse cultures and their changing political and epistemological contexts suggests a different way to understand architecture. Over the centuries and through widely different incarnations and modes of production, this discipline has offered humanity far more than superfluous pleasure or a technical solution to pragmatic necessities.

Our technological world often promotes skepticism about architecture having any meaning other than providing for shelter or functioning as a commodity and status symbol. For a technological mentality, universal truths obtain legitimacy by association with the technical achievements of applied science based on a mathematical language, the one language that seems unquestionable, regardless of local traditions and cultures. Our technological world is one driven almost exclusively by efficiency of means. Efficiency, demonstrable through mathematical argumentation, stands as an absolute value in all orders of life. The means can therefore claim to be unaffected by the social consequence of its ends. This is potentially disastrous for an ethical intentionality. Furthermore, the technological world is one in which specialization is deemed as the only solution to the proliferation of information. To operate efficiently the specialist typically disregards the language of history and the humanities, the source of wisdom that provides an ethical capacity to speak for one's actions in view of a total life experience, here and now.

Misled by technological progress, reason may be capable of dismissing the quality of the built environment as central to our spiritual well-being, yet our dreams and our actions are always set *in place*, and our understanding of others and ourselves would be impossible without significant places. Our bodies can recognize and understand—despite our so-called "scientific" common sense and its Cartesian isotropic space—the wisdom embodied in a place and its profound, untranslatable expressive qualities. With little effort we can recognize how architecture, in those rare places that speak back to us and resonate with our dreams, incites us to meditation, personal thought and imagination, opening up the "space of desire" that allows us to be "at home" while remaining always "incomplete" and open to our most durable human characteristic: personal mortality. Even the seductive binary spaces in our computer screens could not appear to resemble reality if we were not first and foremost mortal, self-conscious bodies, *already* engaged in our world through orientation and gravity. We don't merely have a body; we *are* our bodies, already engaged in our world in mutual dialogue. Our unarticulated, pre-conceptual "ground" of being depends fundamentally upon architecture as the external, visible order that makes our limits present.

Architecture does not communicate *a* particular meaning, but rather the possibility of recognizing ourselves as complete despite our inherent openness as erotic beings, in order to dwell poetically on earth and thus be wholly human. In the Western tradition, the products of architecture have ranged from the *daidala* of classical antiquity to the sundials, machines and buildings that Vitruvius names as the three manifestations of the discipline, from the gardens and ephemeral architecture of the Baroque period to the built and unbuilt "architecture of resistance" of modernity, including a number of projects and architectural objects produced by Henriquez Partners. These objects and spaces are seductive. They destabilize us, like when we fall in love. Socrates often emphasized that this moment, a seemingly irrational state represented by cupid's arrow, was (contrary to the arguments of reason) the true foundation of any knowledge that may be significant for humans. This recognition enabled by architecture is not merely one of semantic equivalence; rather it occurs in experience, and like in a poem, its "meaning" is inseparable from the experience of the poem itself. It is embedded in culture, it is playful by definition, and is always circumstantial. These artifacts, *thaumata*, convey wonder, a form of beauty grounded in *eros* (*Venus-tas* is the word used for beauty by Vitruvius). Architectural beauty, like erotic love, burns itself into our soul, it inspires fear and reverence through a "poetic image," one that affects us primarily through our vision, and yet is fully sensuous, synaes-thetic: it is thus capable of seducing and elevating us to understand our embodied soul's participation in wholeness. What differentiates these artifacts from other forms of *ars* or *poiesis* is their intertwining with life itself in the form of significant action. To be rooted in culture, architecture aims to be appropriate, a form of decorum. Architecture is a *mimesis* of *praxis* (or a representation of ethical human action), in the definition that Aristotle pro-vides for the work of art.

In other words, good architecture offers societies a place for existential orientation. It allows for participation in meaningful action, conveying to the participant an understand-ing of his or her place in the world. Successful architecture opens up a clearing for the individual's experience of purpose through participation in cultural institutions. At its best, it plays with power. The order it conveys, however, is impossible to paraphrase. It is radical orientation in experience, beyond words. Its theory has been rooted in myths, phi-losophy, theology and science throughout history, yet architecture is none of these but an event. It is ephemeral and has the capacity of changing one's life in the vivid present—exactly like an erotic encounter. It embodies knowledge, but rather than clear logic it is a bodily, fully sexual and therefore opaque experience of truth. For this reason, its meaning can never be objectified, reduced to functions, ideological programs, formal or stylistic formulas. Likewise, its technical medium is open rather than specific (like say, building typologies), including all artifacts from diverse media that make possible human dwelling and which by definition stand at the limits of language, establishing the bound-aries of human cultures within which other more properly linguistic forms of expression may take place.

Architecture engages language to frame significant events appropriately. In the best of cases, its main theoretical concern is not instrumental but ethical. The purpose of theory is therefore to find appropriate language (in the form of stories) capable of modulating a project in view of ethical imperatives, always specific to each task at hand. The practice that emerges from such a theory can never be an instrumental application or a totalizing operation, one that might be universally applied as a particular architect's style or method. Rather, this *praxis* aims at the production of harmonious, well-adjusted fragments that may question, by inducing wonder, the hegemony of the ideological, fundamentalist or technological beliefs embedded in the physical fabric of the global village. This *praxis* may be better grasped as a verb, as a process that has inherent value, rather than in terms of its heterogeneous products, as a process that has inherent value. The presence of a well-grounded *praxis*, the trajectory of an architect's words and deeds over time, embodying a responsible, practical philosophy grounded in history, is far more important than the particular aesthetic or functional qualities of a particular work.

The poetic and critical dimension of architecture is not unlike literature and film, addressing the questions that truly matter for humanity in culturally specific terms, revealing an enigma behind everyday events and objects. The cultural specificity of practices in our global village is therefore absolutely crucial. Though technology has already had a homogenizing effect, praxis involves much more than technical means and scientific operations—it concerns values, articulated through the stories that ground acts and deeds in a particular culture. The enduring quality of architecture is essential for the perpetuation of cultures. Values, as emerging in the life-world, are preserved by institutions, and embodied in our physical constructions. These diverse practices, like their accompanying dying languages, are valuable endangered species, and must be preserved.

For the true architect, design cannot be dictated by functions, algorithms, or any sort of compositional method. Since the real issues concerning architecture are never simply technological or aesthetic, architectural design is not "problem-solving," and formal innovation is not enough. Architects engage their imagination to make poetic artifacts rather than plan buildings, employing dimensions of consciousness that are usually stifled by our culture and present educational paradigms. This is not an intuitive operation or unreflective action, but rather the continuation of a practical philosophy and a meditative practice: it is making with an awareness of expectations, in a collaborative mode whenever appropriate to the tasks. For poetry, according to Giambattista Vico, is a kind of metaphysics whose truth speaks to and through the imagination-consciousness, body and memory all in one, rather than in the language of scientific algorithms. Humanity creates, makes poetry, architecture and institutions, but in a way very different from that of God (or modern technology). I quote: "For God, in his purest intelligence, knows things, and by knowing them, creates them; but [humans] in their robust ignorance, [do] it by virtue of a wholly corporeal imagination, one liable to perturb in excess."

In view of these realizations, it is essential to grasp the possible confluence of ethics and poetics in the 21st century. The present excesses of empty computer-generated formalism, with its roots in liberal capitalism, and the far more insidious moral disasters that humanity witnessed during the last century in the name of health and beauty, associated particularly with fascism, but also with communism, have made us justifiably skeptical. I would like to invoke Plato and argue that beauty, as a form of deeply shared cultural experience, understood as a priori *meaning* in the world of culture, is a fundamental category. In *Phaedrus* the experience of beauty is a vehicle for the soul to ascend towards truth, (pt)*eros* provides the wings. Beauty is truth incarnated in the human realm, it is a trace of the light of Being that mortals can seldom contemplate directly, it is the purposefulness of nature mimetically reflected by the artifact. To paraphrase Hans-Georg Gadamer: In this "world below," we can be deceived by what only seems wise, or what merely appears to be good. Even in this world of appearances, however, all beauty is true beauty, because it is in the nature of beauty to appear. This is what makes the beautiful distinct among ideas, according to Socrates. Beauty exemplifies, in Karl Jasper's terms, reason incarnate in existence. This Platonic formulation offers a great challenge, as we must understand it in our epoch of cultural relativism.

It is easy to understand taste as participating in local, historically determined norms. Yet, when we move beyond conventional aesthetics, taste takes its place among other forms of *phronesis*, Aristotle's "practical wisdom" grounded in the habits and values that we share with others and that appear with utmost clarity and certainty. Such self-evidence, manifested in the poetic artifacts and stories of our traditions, can produce judgments that are no less rational for being grounded in ethos. These works of art and poetry are indeed capable of moving us. We may question the motivations behind them and even believe that their effect is illusory. Deconstruction has even tried to reduce it all to homogeneous "writing." Yet, poetic works transform our life and ground our very being; they become hinges revealing a sense of purpose and order in history.

Eros and the imagination are inextricably linked. This is more than a physiological fact. Our love of beauty is our desire to be whole and to be holy, beauty transcends the *aporia* of necessity and superfluity; it is both necessary for reproduction, and crucial for our spiritual well-being, the defining characteristic of our humanity. Richard Kearney, among other philosophers in the hermeneutic tradition, has demonstrated the importance of the imagination for ethical action. Contrary to the view of many critical theorists who may believe that there exists an irreconcilable contradiction between ethics (associated with democracy, rationality and consensus) and the poetic imagination, Kearney convincingly shows how it is the lack of imagination that may be at the root of our worst moral failures. Imagination is precisely our capacity for love and compassion, for both recognizing and valorizing the other, for understanding the other as self, over and above differences of race, gender, culture and belief. Imagination is both our capacity for truly free play, and our faculty to make stories that partake from the language and vision of others.

Architects are called to build the public realm, and their main vehicle is the personal imagination. Rather than a limitation that should be avoided, the imagination is the condition for truly significant work. Architectural works may have enormous consequences.

This obvious observation is actually magnified by our historically given condition. We have inherited a great responsibility, for unlike our ancestors until the seventeenth century we effectively *make* history and believe in the self-evidence of human-generated change towards progress. This is a characteristic of Western culture with its origins in Christianity that has become universalized. Thus history, our diverse stories as varied as our cultures, is what we share as a ground for action, together with an indeterminate and somewhat infirm, more-than human world that appears forever fragmented. We don't share, like our more distant ancestors, a perception of the universe as a fundamentally changeless and limited cosmos. The imagination's capacity to create compassionately is crucial to acknowledge cultural diversity in view of the nearly infinite possibilities for production offered by computer software. The imagination is equally the antidote to the prevailing cynical view about architecture, according to which it matters little what we make, for it will be co-opted by politics and power, its purpose being to exploit, dominate or control the other.

There are, of course, difficulties that emerge from monetary and political interests. Nietzsche has shown us that for this purpose a playful attitude seems to work best. Despite these difficulties, renouncing innovation is not an ethical option for the architect. Our historicity may now reveal the futility of Utopia and the early modern ideal of infinite progress, yet to project inherently means to propose, through the imagination, a better future for a polity. The architectural project is inherently an ethical practice, and this is not equivalent to a mindless search for consumable novelties disconnected from history.

Throughout human history, architecture has often provided authentic dwellings, enabling individuals to recognize their place in a purposeful natural and cultural context. At times, however, particularly during the modern period, buildings have contributed to tragedy. The aesthetic programs underlying Nazi Germany are a case in point. Rather than being underscored by the imagination, the Nazi programs were borne from a rationalized mythology, transformed into the dogma of nationalism. Think as well of the way two very tall yet typical skyscrapers, secular products of a triumphant technology, were read as ideological signs by Muslim fundamentalists on September 11, 2001. The sad event of their destruction transformed two largely conventional buildings into symbols, having a nefarious effect on our world civilization. For all these reasons, we should remember that despite the loss of poetic enchantment in the world as it opens itself to nihilism, all we can do is continue to weaken the strong values of all sorts of ideologies and fundamentalist positions, ranging from organized religion to technology, expecting that in the gaps a new, genuine spirituality may emerge. Truly unethical is to pretend that there exists a unique and absolute set of values to be represented in architecture, articulated in one mythology, dogmatic religion, rational ideology or technology. The most authentic modern architecture opens itself to the abyss. It is meaningful precisely by not functioning as a literal sign: like poetry it operates against prosaic or scientific language. To attain the goal of weakening strong values, an ethical *praxis* in architecture is fragmented, difficult to consume and reduce to fashionable image; every project is carefully contextualized and the design responses are specific, never artificially stylistic. In every circumstance the architect must be prepared with Nietzsche and Heidegger to wait patiently for the rustle of the angels' wings that may be passing by, avoiding the planner's dream of total solutions and the fashion designer's quest for consumable images.

Given the dangers at hand, it is crucial for the architect to develop a language that articulates responsibility and that anchors an inherently ambivalent practice. From its inception in human history, technical production, however poetic, carries a dimension that moves "against nature." It is a necessary danger for *Homo sapiens*, who unlike other animals can never simply adapt themselves to the natural environment: a potential curse which is also one of humanity's most precious gifts, narrated by many myths of traditional cultures, such as the stories of Prometheus and Cain. We may recall the ambivalent nature of the Greek *daidala*, the earliest architectural artifacts in the Western tradition (like Tecton's ship, the labyrinth, the horse of Troy, and Achilles' shield) that were both dangerous and wondrous, eliciting a power of seduction that was also a power of defense against all enemies, deceitful and yet necessary for the survival of the human spirit. Like votive and sacrificial objects, *daidala* were both sacred and polluted. While many of our cultural achievements have been obtained at great cost, it would be naïve to claim that the answer might be to live closer to nature, following the wisdom of our ancestral cultures. For us on the other side of modernity, reading the landscape like an Australian aborigine, or living at one with nature like our mythical ancestors, are not real options. As Heidegger has shown, there is a serious danger for humanity when, as we live our lives in a world of objects that conceal our finite horizon and impede our access and understanding of the more-than-human world, we treat nature as a collection of resources to be exploited. If something has been lost through modernity, such as our cultural understanding of *genius loci*, something has been gained as well. The highly artificial culture within the technological world is now capable, through historical self-consciousness, of embracing the previously contradictory *aporias* of cyclical and linear time in order to recognize the same mysterious origins once discovered and released through the earliest products of *techne-poiesis*. Through historical recollection and future orientation, architects can cultivate a capacity for stewardship and responsibility. They can develop their poetic potential as makers to disclose and celebrate the original mystery as it appears in the primary structure of our embodiment, the meaningfulness of a given world that refuses to be reduced to universal categories.

While the appropriate language (and critical understanding) is therefore crucial for an ethical practice, one should immediately acknowledge that words and deeds never fully coincide; language is opaque. This is not the fault of the architect, and should be celebrated rather than deplored. The opaqueness of language characterizes the very nature of human existence, which is never coincidental with the words of gods for whom "to name is to make." The possession of symbolic, multivocal languages is among the most precious gifts that makes us human, perhaps more precious than our approximations to an ideal, scientific or mathematical universal language. As George Steiner has eloquently stated, human beings are singular among all species for having over three-and-a-half thousand distinct languages capable of poetic expression. *Homo sapiens*, despite living in close proximity, remains linguistically diverse and capable of speaking poetically in ways that through translation may enrich the other's experience of reality: this is the ultimate enigma which no evolutionary theory of man can ever reduce.

No matter what architects produce, once the work inhabits the public realm, it is truly beyond their control. An expressed intention can never fully predict the work's meaning. Others decide its destiny and its final significance. Despite this logical conundrum, the architect's best bet is to understand that there is an inherent phenomenological continuity between thinking and making, between words and deeds. Despite the predominant opinion that often dismisses good intentions in view of "real" deeds, well-grounded intentions are crucial and rare in the modern world. Beyond what an individual architect is capable of articulating at the surface of consciousness, or through one particular project, intentions imply a whole style of thinking and action that takes into account a past life and thick network of connections within a culture. Intentional thinking is the foundation of *praxis*, in the full Aristotelian sense. Once a modern architectural theory is understood as practical philosophy driven by ethics, *techne-poiesis* or practice appears as process, as a fully embodied and open-ended personal engagement with making that is not driven by instrumental concerns or methodologies.

Within a framework of understanding derived from a hermeneutic reading of history, ethics appears not through norms or generalities, but through stories that focus on specific works and individuals. In recent critical theory the self has been portrayed as a dangerous, inflated ego, product of the eighteenth century. Feminist and social critiques have tended to render art and design as the result of more or less anonymous, more or less insidious forces. The unmasking of ego-centered interpretations is healthy. What is very dangerous, however, is to follow up this diagnosis with a desire to renounce the personal imagination in design as if it were some evil, distorting device, in favour of diagrams, algorithms, or a supposedly objective consensual framework. I have already alluded, with Richard Kearney, to the ethical function of the imagination. The imagination is the hinge of ethics and poetics, crucial for seduction and compassion; it is the vehicle to build an architecture upon love, in the sense of both seduction and brotherly affection, as a promise for the common good.

It is always the I who acts, a fully embodied and imaginative first person, caught in a technological and historical world that both endows the architect with responsibility and limits the range of possibilities. The author of architectural projects, fully rooted in language and culture through the medium of the body, is also capable of poetic speech, of making beyond the confines of a narrow style, ideology or nationality. My claim is that individual architects in history, despite the apparent dangers of the imagination and the opaque relationship between words and deeds, have indeed contributed imaginative answers to our universal call for dwelling. Through their personal reformulation of universal, social questions, in view of their own historically and geographically specific framework of beliefs, they have generated poetic responses that embody beauty as the expression of justice.

ALBERTO PÉREZ-GÓMEZ

2006

Bruce Eriksen Place

Coal Harbour Community Centre

Henriquez Family Residence

Bruce Eriksen Place · VANCOUVER, BC 1997

THE STREET FAÇADE of Bruce Eriksen Place bears the message, "Memory, Mother of the Community." Situated near the intersection of Main and Hastings streets, ground zero for Vancouver's open drug scene, the affordable housing project's message courageously proclaims the neighbourhood's spirit of survival. The project's namesake, Bruce Eriksen, died in 1997; he was an anti-poverty activist who served on city council from 1980 to 1993. His social ideals of dignity and respect were inscribed on the building's front balconies and infused in the process of the project's making.

Bruce Eriksen Place was the first of three architectural projects that Gregory Henriquez and Jim Green, then a provincial bureaucrat, worked on together. Conceived by Green, Bruce Eriksen Place not only replaced some of the Downtown Eastside's deteriorated single occupancy units, but also afforded an opportunity to set up the Main and Hastings Housing Society as an alternative to the Downtown Eastside Residents' Association (DERA), Vancouver's primary affordable housing advocacy group. At that time, DERA was proposing to achieve affordability in housing through micro-suites of 19 m², below the minimum 25 m² required by the City of Vancouver for self contained suites. Through Green's advocacy, increased government funding allowed the average unit size at Bruce Eriksen Place to be 40 m². Each of the thirty-five studio apartments has a living room, kitchen, bathroom and a fold-out bed. In addition, residents have access to generous amounts of open space—rooftop gardens and a rear courtyard with blackberry bushes—essential for an area that has few quiet and safe refuges. By providing more than the bare minimum, Bruce Eriksen Place stands as a model for future affordable housing developments.

Gregory's humane approach is most significantly evidenced by the consideration given to poetic expression of the human spirit through architecture, something that most social housing lacks. The front façade is a simple "modernist billboard" that recalls consciousness-raising Soviet agitprop graphics of the 1920s. Above the retail units, a photomontage screen by artist Blake Williams depicts Bruce Eriksen and the 1930s labour marches. A committee of Downtown Eastside residents working directly with Williams chose the words inscribed on the balconies of the front façade. Williams intended that the façade should be "a thorn in the side of those whose priorities negatively affect the community," in contrast to Vancouver's customary unobjectionable developer-sponsored civic art. Henriquez Partners confined themselves to specifying the size, colour palette and typeface for the words on the balconies.

Bruce Eriksen Place reflects the Downtown Eastside community's spirit and a collective remembrance of the roots of that spirit in Bruce Eriksen himself: a man who fought to house a low-income community under the threat of displacement by creeping gentrification and the pressures of poverty.

Coal Harbour Community Centre · VANCOUVER, BC 2000

THE COAL HARBOUR NEIGHBOURHOOD on the north side of Vancouver's downtown peninsula has spectacular views of Stanley Park, Burrard Inlet and the North Shore Mountains. It was developed through a partnership between Marathon Developments and the City of Vancouver to convert former port lands into a dense neighbourhood that supports living, working and leisure. Through a comprehensive rezoning, Marathon and the City negotiated the development's allowable density and required public amenities. A cost-sharing agreement funded Coal Harbour's community centre, park space and parking structure in phase one; a second phase, set to enter design development in 2007, will include an elementary school, daycare and non-market housing.

Typical of Vancouver's downtown residential developments, Coal Harbour's master plan aimed to maximize the distant views captured by its proposed condominium towers and to ensure public access to the waterfront through parks, the community centre and the seawall. The community centre slips underground into a four and a half metre grade change, preserving private views while fulfilling the public mandate of providing unrestricted access to the water's edge.

The community centre's continuity with Coal Harbour's maritime history is established and reinforced through its architectural vocabulary. Organic concrete site work anchors the community centre's buried form, which emerges from the water's edge like a surfacing submarine. The central corridor, penetrated by a yellow conical tower skylight, is designed like the hull of a ship; details such as stainless steel railing further the metaphor. Gregory asserts, "It is the architect's role to give meaning, to elicit a story, where no script exists."

The design of the amphitheatre exemplifies the conflicts of public and private interests presented by the cost-sharing agreement. Jim Lowden of the Vancouver Park Board requested an amphitheatre to support public gatherings and performances. Marathon, Henriquez Partners' direct client, was concerned about disturbances that might be caused by having an amphitheatre adjacent to a luxury tower site. Ben Baron, then Marathon's project manager for the community centre, required Henriquez Partners to explore alternative designs that would discourage gathering. Gregory took inspiration from the rounded belly of his pregnant wife, Zena, and inverted the amphitheatre from a sunken form to a mound, addressing both the Park Board's program and Marathon's concern. Like ancient burial mounds recalling the cycle of death and rebirth, the mound symbolizes Coal Harbour's revitalization from an obsolete industrial site to a dense urban neighbourhood and the reconciliation necessary within any successful community development initiative.

Henriquez Family Residence · VANCOUVER, BC 2003

VANCOUVER IS OFTEN CITED as a successful model of dense urban living that other North American cities aspire to emulate, but the reality is that the city's recent condominium developments are designed for small households with large incomes. New apartments are predominantly one- or two-bedroom units and expensive due to Vancouver's heated real estate market. This makes single-family homes one of the few options for larger families.

In this climate, Zena and Gregory Henriquez embarked on a search for a house to accommodate their growing family. Zena searched daily on internet real estate sites for her dream post-and-beam house until she found the fragments of one, complete with a carport, in the quiet south Vancouver residential neighbourhood of Kerrisdale. The house is situated in the shadow of an ancient cedar tree. The tree's prominent location and protected status discouraged potential developers from demolishing the existing home to build speculative housing.

Built in 1948, the original 150 m² house is one of the first post-and-beam designs by Fred Hollingsworth, an originator of West Coast Modernism in Vancouver. The house is an example of the innovative single-family detached houses built to address housing shortages after World War II. The innovations developed in the West Coast strain of Modernism were desirable for the post-war generation of homeowners who equated modern living with minimalist and cost-effective design. Ample light and space were associated with social freedom, health and well-being. Few interior walls and extensive glazing made possible by the post-and-beam system made houses feel more spacious for those unable to buy more space. While modular like the 1940s Case Study houses of California, Vancouver's West Coast Modern houses expressed an organic disposition through their ample use of indigenous wood and broad roof overhangs.

When Zena and Gregory purchased their house, its beam-ends had been cut off and the interior was dark and moldy. Gregory's renovation intended to improve the design's livability and develop the logic of the post-and-beam style rather than faithfully reproduce the original design. He retained the concrete slab and basic structural elements that could be economically re-used. To support the long roof overhangs, new beam-ends were added using steel rebar and marine epoxy. The tongue-and-groove cedar planks of the original interior partition walls were salvaged, milled and assembled into window frames on site for the new floor-to-ceiling windows; the profile for the window frame was copied directly from the 1950 edition of *Architectural Graphic Standards* to achieve stylistic authenticity. The second floor addition, consisting of three bedrooms and two bathrooms, harmonically repeats the original elements of flat roof, large overhangs, and cedar tongue-and-groove exterior siding.

In light of a current shortage of affordable housing in Vancouver, the social concern that originally inspired the development of affordable post-and-beam houses is still relevant almost half a century later. The Case Study program ended in 1966 in a climate of widespread disillusionment and dismissal of Modernism's ideology as simplistic and utopian. Since that time, a cautious proposition of architecture's relevance in addressing contemporary social needs has resurfaced, tempered by increasing understanding of the complexities involved.

Beauty and Necessity *Jim Green interviewed by Helena Grdadolnik*

IN AN OFFICE located in the former B.C. Electric Railway Company Building (known locally as the Tram Building) at the corner of Hastings and Carrall streets, the heart of Vancouver's Downtown Eastside, Jim Green and I discussed the role of ethics, activism and critical commentary in contemporary architectural practice. Jim has been an activist and advocate for this neighbourhood since he immigrated to Canada in the mid-1970s from the southern United States. In Vancouver he has worked as a social housing developer, an educator, a provincial civil servant and a city councillor.

OPPORTUNITY

Jim Green: *I have a theory that I call "the architecture of opportunity". What this means is that you are not just developing a building or redeveloping a project, the project is a tool to get to a larger goal: the creation of enlightened human beings. Through the process people become highly skilled and knowledgeable and self-contained because they realize they have the ability to effect change in the world around them.*

Helena Grdadolnik: *With Michael Ames you co-founded the Urban Field School for the University of British Columbia's Department of Anthropology, where you had students work with various Downtown Eastside groups on projects directed by the community. Before you started this, UBC and Simon Fraser University were the two most hated organizations in the Downtown Eastside. Why was that the case?*

[People saw] the arrogance of universities coming down here: studying them, taking off and leaving nothing behind. I went back to university because I was sick of seeing people quoted about this community when they knew nothing about it. I thought, well Christ, if I go back as Professor Jim Green, urban anthropologist, that is much different than Jim Green, "cockroach commie."

You also used to teach a UBC course for residents in this area. It was called Humanities 101 and had classes on everything from opera to architecture. Can you tell me how that got started?

1 Earl Shorris. *On the Uses of a Liberal Education: As a Weapon in the Hands of the Restless Poor,* HARPER'S MAGAZINE (September, 1997). p.58

2 Jim Green was instrumental in founding The Four Corners Community Savings Bank located at the corner of Main and Hastings streets in Vancouver; it delivered essential banking services to low-income residents in the Downtown Eastside. Jim Green was the president of the bank when it was in operation from 1996 to 2004.

3 Ken Lyotier started United We Can in 1995 as a self-sustaining enterprise that focuses on creating income and job training opportunities in the Downtown Eastside through its bottle depot and street cleaning services.

4 There are three evaluation categories in the Vancouver Heritage Register: "A," "B" and "C". The designation "A" represents buildings of primary significance, and "C" is the lowest level of registered heritage buildings.

UBC wanted to come to the Downtown Eastside. My students interviewed close to one thousand Downtown Eastsiders and what did they want in their lives? They wanted Humanities 101 and a swimming pool. They wanted all of these things that UBC has. Well the university said, "Here's what you are getting: a computer lab"—which they already had— "used clothing and food." Those last two are utterly insulting to people in this community. That is not what they need. That is typical of the way most things are done: they are imposed from the outside. You need to go to the people themselves and ask what they want instead of making a presumption. ¶ Earl Shorris, a Harper's editor, had a theory that by studying the Humanities people could learn to reason as Socrates could reason and, therefore, low-income people could free themselves from what he called the "surround of poverty." This came to him from a talk he had with a woman from Harlem doing time for murder.[1] ¶ We put together Humanities 101 and the anthropology field school to develop a conscientious group of people down here that really know how to chart a direction for their community and themselves, so that they don't always have to rely on outside experts. They are not architects. I am not an architect. When we need to we will hire an architect, but that architect has to be driven by a similar kind of ideal or it's not going to work.

What was the local response to Humanities 101 and your initiative to hold opera performances in the area?

I was bringing Earl Shorris down from visiting Four Corners Bank[2] to United We Can[3] to visit Ken Lyotier on Hastings Street. There was some hoarding on a building and it opened up and this huge guy came out wearing a leather jacket with no sleeves. He had tattoos everywhere and massive arms; he was obviously a tough cookie. He said to me, "Are you the fucker who runs the bank? Don't fuck around with me, seriously." And I said, "Yeah." Then he continued, "Are you the fucker who brings those operas to the bank?" And I replied, "Yeah, I do." Then he said, "Well, you're a fucking idiot." And I said, "Why is that?" "Well, we haven't had an opera in over two months. When the hell is the next opera? I thought you were the opera guy." You couldn't have asked for better proof that this was working.

INCLUSION

Why do you think that Woodward's, a former department store, became a symbol to people in the area? In some ways it isn't more than a big box store with a dozen poor additions over the years, but it has come to represent something else in the collective imagination.

The Woodward's building is only a "C" on the City's Heritage Register,[4] but its value is tied to the memories it has generated. According to Herbert Muschamp, "A building does not have to be an important work of architecture to become a first-rate landmark ... The essential feature of a landmark is not its design, but the place it holds in a city's memory."[5] I think Woodward's gave a rooted-ness to this community. Everyone has a Woodward's story, even Jane Jacobs. She bought her son his first set of dishes in Woodward's when he got married. Other people who are newcomers and aren't part of that history glom onto it because it has this magnetism, because everyone else has talked about it. It's a reference point. It's a reference to a point in time when people were a lot happier down here. You went in there and you were welcome. You could buy a coffee and a cheap sandwich. You could buy your groceries. I did studies on the food floor. If Woodward's prices were fifteen to twenty percent higher than elsewhere, why would people still shop there? The answer: "Because we feel welcome."

In some ways the Woodward's department store was a successful public space for what was then the financial heart of Vancouver, an indoor public space in a city with a lot of rain. This is something the area no longer has. What's more, so many of the public spaces that we are currently creating in Vancouver are not inclusive; they are not welcoming.

A fence surrounds the public space out here; it can only be looked into, not entered. Woodward's, on the other hand, was a place of interaction.

You referred to the term "spatial apartheid" used by Mike Davis[6] to describe the ghettoes and gated communities in the United States; you said that "this also applies to disabilities, cultural differences, gender, sexual preferences, age, and class affiliations" in Vancouver. Considering that Larry Beasley, the director of current planning in this city for the last twelve years has announced that he is retiring, what do you think are the challenges that his successor will be facing in terms of urban growth and social problems in Vancouver?

In the film Woodward's: The Competition[7] I was amazed by what Larry Beasley said. He said that there are two ways to do redevelopment: one is to drive the poor out physically; another way is to make sure they go quietly into the night and are forgotten. He said we are doing something very different, we are going to be inclusive. We are going to make sure that this project [Woodward's] is for everyone. Which is what we ran on in the last election: "Vancouver for everyone."[8] Jane Jacobs called Larry Beasley the best planner in North America. I think that is a pretty accurate statement. To replace him is difficult because he understands the challenges of Vancouver at a very fine grain. He also travels widely and is very well read. We are going to look internationally for a replacement, but how long is it going to take for someone to catch up with the bloody Olympics coming? Expo '86 really destroyed this neighbourhood. Many people say that Woodward's was the downfall of the small business community in the Downtown

5 "A building does not have to be an important work of architecture to become a first-rate landmark. Landmarks are not created by architects. They are fashioned by those who encounter them after they are built. The essential feature of a landmark is not its design, but the place it holds in a city's memory. Compared to the place it occupies in social history, a landmark's artistic qualities are incidental."
Herbert Muschamp. *The Secret History*, THE NEW YORK TIMES (January 8, 2006).

6 **Mike Davis**. *Ecology of Fear: Los Angeles and the Imagination of Disaster.* RANDOM HOUSE, INC. (Toronto, 1999).

7 **Robert Duncan and Carolyn Schmidt.** *Woodward's: The Competition*, DOCTV, (Vancouver, 2005).

8 In 2005 Jim Green ran for mayor of Vancouver as the head of the Vision Vancouver Party and lost the election by a narrow margin.

Eastside. It was the final blow, but Expo destabilized this neighbourhood. The position that I took to protect this community during the upcoming Olympics [9] was informed by what I had seen happen in the years leading up to Expo.

About the Olympics, do you think that Vancouver is meeting the targets it set for sustainability and inclusiveness as they were laid out in the Olympic bid?

If you think of it, here is the real problem: we talk about sustainability and inclusiveness all the time, but by pronouncing the words we feel that we have accomplished the goal. If you look at our claim that we will have an inclusive Olympics, well, let's look at what has happened. The social housing units and middle-income housing have been reduced on the False Creek Olympic Village site, and there was a ground-breaking to kick off the Olympics where the Governor General got up and gave a talk based on inclusiveness—and the event was closed to the public. It was a nice image that we were working toward, but I'm afraid that the image has become a cardboard cutout.

COMMUNITY DESIGN

You have always worked towards empowering the disenfranchised. As the head of the Downtown Eastside Residents' Association from 1981 to 1991 you were instrumental in building hundreds of units of social housing with a community design model. Why do you think it is important for people to have a voice in building their own communities?

We were not building a product for people to move into. That is the model that you saw at Pruitt-Igoe, [10] at Raymur [11] and at Regent Park in Toronto, [12] which they are now redoing after fifty years of screwing up. People have to be involved in their own decision-making; they need to feel a sense of ownership. With community leadership you have possession: you designed it and chose the purple walls. You don't like the purple walls, too bad. But if you move into a place with purple walls and didn't have anything to do with the decision and you hate it, that is another story. Gropius, and others that came out of the Bauhaus and various Modern movements, were using the idea of sameness to avoid nationalism, which leads to fascism. Now we look at their designs and say, "Good god, that is fascist." They had good intentions, but it didn't work because those Modernists weren't talking to people to find out their needs, desires and dreams. ❡ A quick example: at Four Sisters Co-op you have seventy-five kids in the heart and soul of the murder district of Canada—the heroin district, prostitution, AIDS, tuberculosis, et cetera—living in utter harmony and the reason is that their mothers understood their needs. If you go to the Mau Dan Co-op just a few blocks away, you will find that every family housing

9 The Downtown Eastside Residents' Association tried to pass a single occupancy by-law in 1984 to stop mass evictions in the years leading up to Expo '86 in Vancouver. The by-law was finally passed twenty years later in 2004 to ensure that the 2010 Olympic Winter Games will not result in any further evictions.

10 The Pruitt-Igoe Housing Project in St. Louis, Missouri was a housing project designed by Minoru Yamasaki, completed in 1956 and demolished in 1972. It is often used as an example of the failure of modernist planning.

11 Raymur Place Housing Project was built in the 1960s (as part of Vancouver's 1958 Redevelopment Plan) on the opposite side of a rail track from the local elementary school. In 1971 a group of mothers from the social housing—tired of getting nowhere with years of letter writing and petitions—protested on the tracks and stopped traffic to the busy port. Jim Green's wife Roberta McCann was one of the mothers. The women finally succeeded in getting a walkway built over the tracks so that their children could safely walk to school.

12 Regent Park in Toronto, begun in the late 1940s, was the first major social housing project in Canada. The current buildings will be demolished and rebuilt over the next decade as part of the Regent Park Revitalization Plan.

unit has its own private patio with an eight foot high wall around it. If you walk through it you see no joy, no beauty, no children playing, laughing or getting into trouble. When you go through the Four Sister's Co-op, it is mayhem: kids playing everywhere and very few parents around because it is designed with the family units facing inward so that the moms, we call them the courtyard moms, can keep an eye on things. The courtyard moms are primarily single parents. They often set up a night where two or three mothers take care of all the kids so that the others can go to a movie, have a night out or date somebody—actually have an adult life. The architecture is a conduit to help people build a new relationship with themselves and their communities.

Quoting Glen Murray, a former mayor of Winnipeg, you said that necessity and beauty are co-conspirators for social change.[13] *That is a powerful statement. How does this concept apply to architecture and, more specifically, to social housing projects?*

We have seen a legion of examples of architectural hubris and the consequences delivered to the resident and the social fabric. The Pruitt-Igoe complex in St. Louis is the classic example of imposed design on a voiceless people. Pruitt-Igoe was blown up after a few years of dehumanizing occupancy. This trend continues. We have recently witnessed the uprising of people locked in a Corbusian vision morphed into a French nightmare. Of course there are many factors that led to this extreme discontent, including unemployment, racism and poverty, but off-the-shelf design of the suburban or "banlieu" housing projects where the French riots began [in 2005] certainly was a major contributing factor.[14] ¶ The French concept of laïcité is a radical secularism that is blind to race, colour and creed; it also denies the celebration of diversity that gives many cities such as Vancouver their defining culture. A community such as Vancouver's Downtown Eastside that is steeped in poverty, mental illness and drug abuse is also very creative and diverse. For this community to prosper and recognize the value of all its citizens it must recognize and utilize various cultural concepts from Feng Shui to medicine wheels. This enables a new culture to emerge that is characterized by the unity of diversity.

You have been a significant figure in plotting the course of the Woodward's redevelopment project for well over a decade. How does Woodward's compare to typical development projects? Do you see it as a new model for development in North American cities?

Woodward's is a project that started as a community development dream and it has become the biggest single site development in the history of Vancouver. It is a landmark project that is very different than any other major project in the city because it was created out of social concern. A project like Shangri-La[15] can generate social good from private interests, but Woodward's

13 In a presentation at the Creative Places + Spaces Conference held in Toronto October 17-18, 2003 Glen Murray said, "Make the beauty necessary and the necessary beautiful." He attributed this idea to Winnipeg landscape architect Garry Hilderman.

14 Triggered by the deaths of two teenagers in Clichy-sous-Bois (a poor suburb of Paris consisting of the social housing hi-rises typical of France and inspired by le Corbusier's Ville Radieuse), a series of riots began on October 27, 2005 involving predominantly second-generation immigrant youth from underprivileged neighbourhoods burning cars and public buildings.

15 Currently under construction with an expected completion date of 2008, the Shangri-La will be Vancouver's tallest tower, home to North America's first Shangri-La hotel and some of the most expensive condominiums per square foot in the city to date. Westbank Projects and Peterson Investment Group, the same companies involved in the Woodward's redevelopment, are behind the development.

turned this upside down. Social good drove the private sector into doing the project and the Downtown Eastside has rallied behind it. There is no opposition to Woodward's that I have encountered. How can you do a two hundred and fifty million-dollar project in the poorest community in Canada without having an uprising? The fact is that it is based on a model of inclusiveness that people believe is real. They have been involved in it so they know it's real. Jane Jacobs once said, "The good thing about getting older is we get to see how things work out." I believe Woodward's will turn out to be a sonnet to inclusivity.

THE ARCHITECT IN SOCIETY

In contemporary North American society the role of the architect is often defined quite narrowly —as a spatial designer, a fashion designer or a building envelope engineer. How should the role of the architect be defined? And how can the role of the architect be redefined to include society and the community more directly?

When I was working for the provincial government I came up with a concept called Hip Hop, short for "housing is priority in honing our potentials." The idea was to create housing that would be developed, designed, built, occupied and managed by young people. When we put out an advertisement for an architect, the ability to work with young, low-income people was listed as one of the necessary skills. There was a steering committee of young people and the chair was a nineteen year-old prostitute who was nine months pregnant. She had a ring in her nose, a shaved head and probably the lowest cut top you have ever seen on a pregnant woman. When the architects that we had short-listed would come in for the meeting I would introduce myself and I would introduce them to Sarah saying, "This is our chair." She sat at one end of the boardroom and I sat at the other. Almost every one of them turned and presented to me. When Gregory Henriquez came in, he presented to Sarah. ¶ He understood what we were doing. Those people [the end users] were the decision makers, not me. They were going to be directing the project, not me. Most people couldn't get around that; they have an old way of thinking. Gregory is representative of a new way of working, a dialectical engagement between the architect and society. It is not the major trend. The major trend is for architectural consultants to become the instruments of private interest rather than meaningfully engaging with society and participating in the development of communities. So that means, What style is the style of the month? I want a Gehry. I want a Gehry. And that's how we got one hundred Gehrys all over the world that look pretty much alike. And some of them are utter crap, like the Experience [Music Project] in Seattle. It should be taken out and dragged behind a pick-up until its dead.

It looks like it already has been.

I think you're right. Anyway, for community projects, it is imperative that the architects understand who their client is and be able to get along with them. They have to understand that low-income people have ethics; they have aspirations; they have a code of conduct; they have an idea of beauty. They are dying to learn. Give us bread, but give us roses. That's where the architect has to help; they have to have flexibility to understand the community. If you look at the design of the projects that are driven from the top, they often fail. Then take a look at the ones where the community has been involved and you get award-winning projects. The people that are going to be using the building are the ones that know what they want. They may not know how to take it from idea and wish to reality—that is the bridge that the architect should bring.

The project that Gregory [Henriquez] was chosen for later evolved to become Bruce Eriksen Place. This was the first of three projects that you and he worked on together. Can you tell me about it?

Bruce Eriksen was dying [16]. The idea was, How do you develop this [building] so that it is not just a monument to a person? We wanted it to be alive. I don't know where the idea of putting the words up came from; I think it was probably Gregory, in all fairness, [17] but community members chose the words. That is what makes them so significant. By having the words up and having the history of Bruce Eriksen embedded into the façade of the building it changed the project from "Bruce is a hero," which he is, to "This is what it takes to build a community." It takes "courage" and "commitment" and "work" and "hope." However, the City of Vancouver proclaimed it contravened the sign by-law and the words were to be removed. After an appeal, the City finally agreed that it wasn't a sign but a poetic investigation. ¶ Bruce Eriksen Place became one of the most significant buildings in the city because of that community involvement and because of Gregory's input. Again I have to clarify this: I don't think the architect is a whipping boy to bring in. We got the most talented possible person with the most to give and began the project with the understanding that it was a partnership. I think Bruce Eriksen Place shows a real marriage between art and necessity. Someone living in the building said to me, "Since I've lived here I'm going nuts because the balcony above me is 'Home' and mine is 'Work' so I have to do all my Humanities 101, I can't go to sleep without doing my homework."

Once again you mention a connection between beauty (or art) and necessity. The Greeks believed that beauty and ethics were inseparable; Plotinus said, "all the virtues are a beauty of the soul," [18] but today we often consider beauty and ethics or beauty and necessity as distinct concepts. Can you elaborate on how you believe the two are related?

16 Bruce Eriksen, a seaman and ironworker, became a Downtown Eastside community activist and a Vancouver City Councillor.

17 Gregory Henriquez approached the artist Blake Williams with the idea of doing a community art collage for the entire Bruce Eriksen Place façade. Due to the allotted budget, Blake Williams said it would not be possible to have images over the entire elevation, but that they could use words instead and keep any imagery within the lower portion of the façade.

18 Plotinus. Translated by Stephen Mackenna and B.S. Page. The *First Ennead. Sixth Tractate: Beauty*, THE SIX ENNEADS. Written ca. 250 A.D.

Beauty and the struggle for inclusion are not contradictory. Take, for example, Dr. Martin Luther King Jr.'s famous "I Have a Dream" speech. The message of liberation is delivered within the most beautiful poetry. The speech would not have had as great an impact if either the message or the poetry had been presented in isolation. ¶ Let's look at an example of Gregory's work: the Gastown Parkades. Function and beauty intertwine. Parking garages are usually dark, unsafe and unattractive places, but this parkade shimmers with a palate of vibrating colours; unexpected views of the mountains and the city create layers of meaning and sensations never anticipated in a parking structure. I think the night that I first really got off on the building was the night of the balloons,[19] when I drove Heather Redfern, the head of the Greater Vancouver Alliance for Arts and Culture, around the Parkade and looked at all the pastels. It's this real slap in the face of utilitarianism. And it says: it works, it's beautiful. It works. It's beautiful.

Vancouver • 3 April 2006

19 On August 18, 2005 the opening party for Space-Agency's FrontierSpace was held in the alley behind the Gastown Parkades. Frontier-Space was an international competition to rethink the Gastown alleyways with a temporary installation. The winning entry by Satoshi Matsuoka and Yuki Tamura consisted of large white balloons.

LORE KRILL HOUSING CO-OP

GASTOWN PARKADES

WOODWARD'S REDEVELOPMENT

Lore Krill Housing Co-op · VANCOUVER, BC 2002

LORE KRILL HOUSING CO-OP was birthed out of a decade-long struggle between private and public interests over the fate of the derelict Woodward's department store. The provincial government set aside funding for two hundred non-market housing units for the Woodward's redevelopment, with an equal number of market units planned. Unable to settle a partnership agreement with Fama Holdings, the developer who had bought the Woodward's building after its closure, the Province permitted the Woodward's Co-op to redirect the funding for the non-market housing offsite in 1997.

As the demolition of Woodward's seemed imminent, Lore Krill's façade was designed to retain a memory of the department store and tell the story of the Co-op's genesis. Lore Krill's brick piers, Chicago-style tri-partite windows and simple cornices emulate the Woodward's façade. Three variations of red bricks were arranged in a basket-weave pattern with slight shifts in sill heights, window sizes, and column widths to evoke Woodward's growth through eight additions over fifty-four years.

Henriquez Partners used a workshop process involving housing consultant Terra Housing and the founders of the Co-op to design Lore Krill. The Co-op members were introduced to building development issues so that they could make informed design and management decisions. The result is a building that challenges current standards of social housing provision. As the Co-op desired a building that could accommodate residents with physical impairments and adjust to the needs of residents as they aged, more than half the units are adaptable, much higher than the typical ten percent. While typical Vancouver housing design is preoccupied with capturing views for private enjoyment, Lore Krill's design has living roofs with gardens for growing vegetables and decks with a variety of outlooks to the city and landscape, accessible to all residents. A landscaped courtyard with gardens, a waterfall and a series of bridges link the two eight-story buildings.

BC Housing's allotted budget was based on a maximum unit price and unwritten modesty guidelines that limit the level of amenity and beauty. The Co-op agreed to reduce individual unit size by ten percent to gain space for shared facilities and a higher standard of materials and finishes. As a result of the communal amenities, the Co-op offers better quality living spaces for the residents than many market housing projects, whose method of pre-sales reduces units to a formula of views, luxury fixtures and finishes, while rendering less tangible aspects of housing design—such as habitable spaces and construction quality—secondary. In the case of the Lore Krill Co-op, a participatory design process ensured that the residents' homes were based on expressed wishes rather than formulaic models; the resulting building questions the predominant models of both social and market housing offered in Vancouver.

Lore Krill, the housing co-op's namesake, was an active resident of the Downtown Eastside and helped found the Main and Hastings Housing Society, Four Corners Community Savings Bank, and Bruce Eriksen Place. After her death in 1999, the Woodward's Co-op was renamed the Lore Krill Housing Co-op in honour of her dedication to community participation, rehabilitation through humane urban living, and housing the most disadvantaged in our society.

Gastown Parkades · VANCOUVER, BC 2004

IN RECENT YEARS, Gregory's work has increasingly been concentrated in the Downtown Eastside, within blocks of Henriquez Partners' office. Once a vibrant hotel and warehousing district, Gastown experienced a decline when commercial activity shifted westward and Woodward's department store closed. The City of Vancouver adopted several initiatives for the Downtown Eastside, including revitalization projects for Gastown, Strathcona and Victory Square, to bring street-level retail businesses back to the area and reduce drug-related crime. In 1995, the City bought the Woodward's Parkade for redevelopment, to provide additional off-street parking and stimulate revitalization of the area.

The project brief asked for the design to be sensitive to its turn-of-the century surroundings, but due to the lack of nineteenth century models of parking structures, Henriquez Partners' design aimed to bridge the values of the past and the needs of the future. The Gastown Parkades consist of two mid-block concrete structures separated by Trounce Alley; one on Water Street, Gastown's main thoroughfare, and the other on Cordova Street, directly across from the old empty Woodward's building. At Gregory's suggestion, new office space was inserted into a fifteen-foot wide strip cut off the front of the existing Water Street structure, to provide streetscape continuity and eyes on the street. Two-and-a-half levels of parking were added to the top of the existing structure while retail and theatre uses were introduced at grade to stimulate street-level activity. The elevation echoes the saw-tooth massing across the street and the principal stair emulates neighbourhood fire escapes. To discourage crime and illicit activity, the stairwells were left open and located in plain view of the street.

The program of theatre, retail and parking extends under Trounce Alley to the new Cordova Street structure. Concrete shear walls, usually found in the centre of parking structures were located around the perimeter to accommodate a central light well and a green filtration bed for cleaning storm water run-off. An intricate lattice of granite and steel, inspired by nineteenth century train stations, screens the exterior of the Cordova parking structure. Black, red and white granite slab "tombstones" mark the buildings previously on the site, the brick piers of the old Woodward's store and the heritage buildings that once existed across the street.

A competition organized by SpaceAgency, a group of young architects led by Helena Grdadolnik, asked entrants to design an installation to temporarily transform the alleys in Gastown. Tokyo architects Matsuoka and Tamura won with a submission that compressed giant balloons between the parkades in Trounce Alley. Constructed in the summer of 2005, the installation heightened the spatial qualities of the buildings and the translucent white spheres played off the vibrant hues of the new structures.

The redevelopment of the Gastown Parkades expresses both progressive optimism for the future revitalization of Gastown and respect for Gastown's unique historic identity. It underscores the City's commitment to long-term investment in the recovery of Vancouver's declining neighbourhoods. With provision for a future pedestrian connection over Cordova Street to the Woodward's building, the Gastown Parkades point to the redevelopment of Woodward's as the practical and symbolic key for addressing economic problems in the Downtown Eastside.

Woodward's Redevelopment · VANCOUVER, BC 2006

IN 1903, CHARLES WOODWARD expanded his mail order catalogue service into a department store built at the corner of Hastings and Abbott streets. By the mid 1950s, Woodward's had defined one-stop shopping in Vancouver: customers could make travel bookings, cash cheques and buy men's and women's fashions. For its low- and modest-income neighbours, Woodward's provided a food floor and other household necessities. The advent of the suburban shopping mall in the 1970s, however, marked the beginning of the store's decline. In 1993, shortly after its one-hundredth anniversary, Woodward's declared bankruptcy and closed its doors.

The demise of Woodward's crystallized a sense of dispossession already felt by many in the Downtown Eastside. By 2001, after many failed attempts to develop Woodward's, the provincial government lost interest and attempted to offload it to a private developer, resulting in "Woodsquat," a protest encampment that surrounded Woodward's from September to December of 2002. Fueled by a decade of advocacy led by Jim Green, then a city councillor, Vancouver's newly elected city council acquired the Woodward's property from the province in March 2003. The purchase was contingent upon the left-leaning council's endorsement of the Vancouver 2010 Olympic Bid that it had originally opposed. The City facilitated an extensive public consultation process of workshops, open houses and meetings, which generated guiding principles for a developer design competition.

Gregory Henriquez assembled a project team, which included developer Westbank Projects/ Peterson Investment Group and community advisor PHS Community Services. The team collaborated in a lengthy two-stage competition and in September 2004 was awarded the Woodward's redevelopment project. Gregory negotiated with the City of Vancouver on behalf of the developer and consulted with community groups throughout the design process with the goal of maintaining the project's financial feasibility while meeting the neighbourhood's social needs. Henriquez Partners orchestrated public and private sector resources to fulfill the needs and desires of all stakeholders, expanding the mandate of the architect to encompass spheres of activity not typically considered to be the architect's responsibility.

Woodward's multi-faceted program includes the diverse elements necessary for a healthy, liveable neighbourhood. The project consists of Simon Fraser University's Centre for the Contemporary Arts, major grocery and drug stores, small retail establishments, two hundred social housing units, over five hundred market condominiums, federal government offices, City non-profit spaces, a daycare, a public indoor atrium, and an outdoor public plaza. To contribute meaningfully to the preservation of Woodward's history and the neighbourhood's heritage character, the project integrates fragments of the existing building within the new scheme. Planted exterior façades and roofs give poetic expression to the project's commitment to sustainability on a large urban scale.

While architecture alone cannot effect deep social transformation, an architect's willingness to engage communities on their own terms can bestow life-changing dignity and respect, redress dispossession, and inspire those facing challenges. What is instructive about Woodward's is the aspiration, repeatedly expressed by the Downtown Eastside's marginalized residents, not only

for housing, but also for a sense of belonging. It is this basic human yearning for orientation and identity that must guide the architect's leadership in shaping the collective spaces of our society.

The Woodward's project challenges today's architects to become *citizen architects*, a term Rural Studio founder Samuel Mockbee used to describe those who "participate in the social, political and environmental realities our communities are facing." He believed that this "requires architects to look beyond architecture towards an enhanced understanding of the whole to which it belongs." [1] Rather than a new or optional role, the *citizen architect* is a fulfillment of the responsibilities already outlined in the *Architect's Oath*, a promise that "my professional conduct as it concerns the community, my work, and my fellow architects will be governed by the ethics and tradition of this honourable and learned profession."

Gregory's search for orientation and meaning undertaken over the last twenty-four years has advanced his praxis of ethics, poetry, critical commentary and community engagement. Whether Woodward's can be counted as a successful model of ethical urban renewal will be revealed over time. Through his active participation in the complex political, economic and social dimensions of Woodward's redevelopment, Gregory Henriquez has charted a course for how today's architects can move beyond complacency, towards an ethical architecture.

1 **Samuel Mockbee.** *"The Role of the Citizen Architect."* *Good Deeds, Good Design: Community Service Through Architecture.* ED. BRIAN BELL. NEW YORK: PRINCETON ARCHITECTURAL PRESS, 2004. 155-6.

Acknowledgements

The making of any building requires the effort of many people. The intention of the project credits is to recognize the invaluable contributions of all the participants.

FIREHALL TRAINING TOWER

Alan Endall
Gregory Henriquez
Richard Henriquez
Earl Lieske
C.Y. Loh
Don Taylor

ARTS UMBRELLA

Paul Ackerson
Peter Brauer
Jaime Dejo
David Harding
Carol Henriquez
Gregory Henriquez
Richard Henriquez
C.Y. Loh
Fred Markowsky
Rui Nunes
Stuart Roy
Lisa Sorensen
Shawn Strasman
Don Taylor

FALSE CREEK COMMUNITY CENTRE

Carol Arnston
Chris Barber
Jaime Dejo
Paul Fast
Gregory Henriquez
Richard Henriquez
Paul Henry
C.Y. Loh
Fred Markowsky

Jason Martin
John Maxey
James Meschino
Jim Nicholls
Rui Nunes
Rudy Roelofsen
Carol Sogawa
Don Taylor

BELLA BELLA COMMUNITY SCHOOL

David Gladstone
Cameron Halkier
Gregory Henriquez
Richard Henriquez
C.Y. Loh
Fred Markowsky
Jim Nicholls
Marie Odile Marceau
Nigel Page
Lisa Sorensen

BRUCE ERIKSEN PLACE

Kathleen Boyes
Jaime Dejo
Jim Green
Monica Haye
Gregory Henriquez
Lore Krill
Jenny Kwan
Fred Markowsky
Jim O'Dea
Shawn Strasman
Blake Williams
Suzann Zimmering

COAL HARBOUR COMMUNITY CENTRE

Ben Baron
Jaime Dejo
John Green
Bruce Hemstock
Gregory Henriquez
C.Y. Loh
Jim Lowden
Fred Markowsky
James Meschino
Rui Nunes
Rudy Roelofsen
Ralph Segal
Lisa Sorensen
Graeme Stamp
Frank Stebner
Shawn Strasman
Gret Sutherland
Yijin Wen
Don Wuori

HENRIQUEZ FAMILY RESIDENCE

Gregory Henriquez
Zena Henriquez
Shadi Jianfar
Shawn Lapointe
Richard Lemaire
Ian MacDonald
C.C. Yao

Lore Krill Housing Co-op

Kathleen Boyes
Jaime Dejo
Geoff Glotman
Cameron Gray
Jim Green
Roland Haebler
Gregory Henriquez
Darren Kitchen
Dana Locke
John Maki
Fred Markowsky
Jason Martin
Ellen Scobie
Frank Stebner
Shawn Strasman
Stuart Thomas

Gastown Parkades

Jaime Dejo
Scot Hein
Gregory Henriquez
Clyde Hosein
Sandy Jung
Shawn Lapointe
Fred Markowsky
Christian Schimert
Frank Stebner
Shawn Strasman
Gret Sutherland
Kevin Wharton
Peter Wood
C.C. Yao

Woodward's Redevelopment

Artour Adamovitch
Larry Beasley
Larry Campbell
Damon Chan
John Cheng
Michelle Corday
Michelle Counihan
Beth Davies
Lee Donohue
Stan Douglas
Liz Evans
Holly Fales
Michael Flanigan
Julie Foxall
Lee Gavel
Michael Geller
Warren Gill
Ian Gillespie
Geoff Glotman
Martin Gotfrit
Jim Green
Cameron Gray
Scot Hein
Gregory Henriquez
Alison Higginson
Clyde Hosein
K.C. Jones
Hal Kalman
Kiky Kambylis
Jake Kearsley
Shawn Lapointe
Tom Lavoilette
Thomas Lee

David Leung
Fred Markowsky
Phil Mondor
Allan Moorey
Bob Nicklin
Jim O'Dea
Michael O'Keefe
Betty Quon
Gene Radvenis
Bob Rennie
Judy Rogers
Erik Roth
Christian Schimert
Ellen Scobie
Rick Scobie
Heather Scott
Dan Small
Greg Smallenberg
May So
Jeffrey Staates
Frank Stebner
Michael Stevenson
Jon Stovell
Ivo Taller
Christine Tapp
James Tod
Michael Toolan
Mark Townsend
Terry Tremayne
Paul Tubbe
Fredy Urrego
David Weir
Phoebe Wong
Peter Wood
Sarah Yada
Ben Yeung

This book is dedicated to the boundless love of Zena Sihota Henriquez.

Notes on Contributors

ALBERTO PÉREZ-GÓMEZ is Saidye Rosner Bronfman Professor at McGill University School of Architecture, chair of the History and Theory of Architecture division and Director of Post-Professional Programs. Born in Mexico City, he obtained his undergraduate degree in architecture and engineering at the National Polytechnic Institute in Mexico City, did postgraduate work at Cornell University and received a Master of Arts and PhD from the University of Essex in England. From 1983 to 1986, he was Director of Carleton University's School of Architecture. He has taught at universities in Mexico City, Houston, Syracuse, and Toronto, and at the Architectural Association in London. His articles have been published in many periodicals including the Journal of Architectural Education, AA Files, Arquitecturas Bis, Section A, VIA, Architectural Design, ARQ, SKALA, A+U, and Perspecta. For his book Architecture and the Crisis of Modern Science (MIT Press, 1983), Dr. Pérez-Gómez was awarded the Alice Davis Hitchcock Award, an annual prize recognizing the most distinguished work of scholarship in architectural history published by a North American scholar. Other books include Polyphilo or the Dark Forest Revisited (MIT, 1992), Architectural Representation and the Perspective Hinge (MIT Press, 1997), co-authored with Louise Pelletier, and CHORA: Intervals in the Philosophy of Architecture (McGill-Queen's University Press), a series Dr. Pérez-Gómez co-edits, which explores fundamental questions of architectural practice through history and theory. His most recent book is Built upon Love: Architectural Longing and Aesthetics (MIT Press, 2006), which uncovers the relationship between poetics and ethics in architecture. Currently, Dr. Pérez-Gómez is engaged in a project to redefine the nature of architectural education by revisiting its historical sources during the Enlightenment and the early 19th century, an imperative task in light of the failures of globalization revealed in the events of September 2001.

JIM GREEN is a local politician, community activist, and Professor of Anthropology at the University of British Columbia where he co-founded the UBC Anthropology Urban Field School. Born in Alabama, he was active in the civil rights movement prior to immigrating to Canada. He studied at numerous institutions including the University of South Carolina, the Sorbonne, the Millennium Film Institute in New York, and the University of Colorado. He holds an MA in Anthropology from the University of British Columbia. In 1981, he joined the Downtown Eastside Residents' Association and spearheaded the development of six hundred new units of social housing. As a provincial bureaucrat, Green was responsible for BladeRunners, a project that provides trade apprenticeships for teenagers on welfare, and represented British Columbia in the National Homelessness Initiative. He has served on various committees including the Counting the Homeless National Steering Committee and the Vancouver Opera Association Outreach Committee. In 1996, he established the Four Corners Community Savings Bank for low-income people, which was closed in 2004 as a result of a new provincial government that did not share its objectives. From 2002 to 2006, he was chair of the Social Economic Development Committee, co-chair of the National Housing Options Team and chair of the Arts, Culture and Heritage of the Federation of Canadian Municipalities. Elected from the COPE party as a Vancouver city councillor in 2002, he was narrowly defeated for mayor in 2005 under his newly formed party, Vision Vancouver.

CHRISTOPHER GRABOWSKI is a Vancouver-based documentary photographer. His photographs have appeared in The Globe and Mail, Washington Post, Financial Times, El Mundo, Utne Reader, Neue Zurcher Zeitung, MacLean's, and Geist. He has exhibited in Canada, Holland, Germany and Poland. Among his several awards in photojournalism is the Michener-Deacon Fellowship, Canada's premier award for investigative journalism serving the public interest. Of his many photo essays, Grabowski's Facing the Downtown Eastside (1998) is notable for its striking portraits of Downtown Eastside residents set in a derelict bank building. As a founding member of Narrative 360, a Canadian non-profit organization for documentary arts, Grabowski photographed war-torn Afghanistan in 2003 for the acclaimed collaborative exhibit, Kites, Guns and Dreams.

HELENA GRDADOLNIK received a Masters degree in architecture from the University of Waterloo in 2002 and is currently pursuing her interest in architectural policy through doctoral studies at the London School of Economics' Cities Programme. She has taught history and theory at the Emily Carr Institute of Art and Design and the University of British Columbia's School of Architecture and Landscape Architecture. Grdadolnik was a founding member of SpaceAgency, an organization dedicated to making space for architecture in the public realm; from 2003 to 2006 she was the Vancouver correspondent for Canadian Architect magazine; and in 2005 was awarded a grant from the Canada Council for the Arts to write a series of articles on architecture for The Tyee, www.tyee.ca.

MAY SO is originally from Hong Kong and worked for architecture firms in Calgary and Vancouver before joining the staff of Henriquez Partners Architects in 2002. She received a Bachelors of Fine Arts at the University of Calgary and a Masters of Architecture from the University of British Columbia. Her work has appeared in several publications including the Journal of Architectural Education, 306090 and The Next American City. For the 2004 Portland Living Smart Competition, her design of a modular infill house prototype received a Design Excellence Award. She has volunteered at various organizations in the Downtown Eastside and her current research lies in the interconnection between poverty, homelessness, and urban governance.

Selected Publications

AUTHORED PUBLICATIONS

Henriquez, Gregory. *Alephville.* Ottawa, 1986. A privately published research thesis from Carleton University. This book embodies architectural ideas in literary form, using film script techniques and theories from contemporary cinema.

——. "Alephville". *Carleton Folio*, No.2. EDS. MARTIN BRESSANI AND G. MITCHELL HALL. Ottawa: Carleton University, 1987. 10-13.

——. "En Soph." *Carleton Folio*, No.2. EDS. MARTIN BRESSANI AND G. MITCHELL HALL. Ottawa: Carleton University, 1987. 44-48.

——. "The Endless Phenomenal Space of Frederick Kiesler." *The Fifth Column* 7, NO. 3 (1990): 18-21.

——. "House for the Traveller." *Directed Studies Abroad: Japan.* EDS. KATSU MURAMOTO AND STEPHEN PARCELL. Ottawa: Carleton University School of Architecture, 1986. 8-11.

Henriquez, Gregory, and Richard Henriquez. "The Ethics of Narrative at Trent University." *Architecture, Ethics and Technology.* EDS. LOUISE PELLETIER AND ALBERTO PÉREZ-GÓMEZ. Montreal: McGill Queen's Press, 1994. 189-198.

PROFESSIONAL PUBLICATIONS

Berelowitz, Lance. *Dream City: Vancouver and the Global Imagination.* Vancouver: DOUGLAS & MCINTYRE, 2005. 103, 212-213. References Coal Harbour Community Centre and Lore Krill Housing Co-op.

Bernstein, William and Ruth Cawker. "Coquitlam Firehall Training Centre." *Contemporary Canadian Architecture: The Mainstream and Beyond.* Markham, Ontario: FITZHENRY AND WHITESIDE, 1988. 211-13.

Boddy, Trevor. "Plastic Lion's Gate." *Vancouver: Representing the Postmodern City.* Vancouver: ARSENAL PULP PRESS, 1993. 25-49. About Firehall Training Tower and history of Henriquez Partners.

City of Vancouver Planning Department. "Coal Harbour: Marathon Lands." *Vancouver's New Neighborhoods: Achievements in Planning and Urban Design.* Vancouver: CITY OF VANCOUVER, 2003. 27-33. About Coal Harbour Community Centre.

Grdadolnik, Helena. "Crosstown Examined." *Canadian Architect* 51, NO. 1 (January 2006): 20-25. About the Woodward's Redevelopment Project.

——. "Putting Housing into Context." *Canadian Architect* 48, NO. 4 (April 2003): 20-23. About Dockside Live/Work Building and Lore Krill Housing Co-op.

——. "Woodward's Takes Shape: Nothing Like it in North America." *The Tyee.* Vancouver, 30 March 2006. Online newspaper article. 24 May 2006. <http://thetyee.ca/Views/2006/03/30/WoodwardsTakesShape/>

Henriquez and Partners Architects. "Design for Leisure: Children's Arts Umbrella." *Canadian Architect* 36, NO. 4 (April 1991): 24-27.

——. "Engaging the Old: False Creek Community Centre." *Canadian Architect* 37, NO.10 (October 1992): 38-39.

——. "Firehall and Training Centre." *Canadian Architect* 34, NO. 4 (April 1989): cover, 36-40.

Henriquez Partners Architects. "Lore Krill Co-op Housing." *Canadian Architect* 49, NO. 5 (May 2004): 42-43.

Matuk, Nyla. "Urban Housing Street Poetry." *Canadian Architect* 44, NO. 8 (August 1999): cover, 22-23. About Bruce Eriksen Place.

Milojevic, Michael. "Spirited Architecture: British Columbia." *Architecture New Zealand* (March/April 1995): 96. About Bella Bella Community School.

Olson, Sheri. "Coal Harbour Community Centre." *Architectural Record* 190, NO.3 (March 2002): 124-127.

Owen, Graham. "The Meaning of Construction, the Construction of Meaning." *Architecture Canada 1994: The Governor General's Awards for Architecture*. GRAHAM OWEN, ED. OTTAWA: THE ROYAL ARCHITECTURAL INSTITUTE OF CANADA, 1994. 32-57.

Rochon, Lisa. "The Re-Generation: How Original Thinkers Are Redefining the Power of Architecture." *Insite Architecture and Design* (September 1994): 39-42. About Allegory Productions, a partnership between Gregory Henriquez and Alex Feldman to design light fixtures.

————. "Vancouver's Street Smarts." *Globe and Mail* (Toronto) 24 September, 2003: R1. About the Gastown Parkades.

Royal Architectural Institute of Canada. "Lore Krill Housing Co-op and City of Vancouver Parkade." *Architecture Canada 2004: The Governor General's Medals in Architecture*. Halifax: TUNS PRESS, 2004. 42-51.

"School Revives Tradition and Looks to the Future." Progressive Architecture 75 (May 1994). About Bella Bella Community School.

Shotton, Elizabeth. "Taking in the View." *Canadian Architect* 46, NO.4 (April 2001): 20-25. About Coal Harbour Community Centre.

Watson, Heather. "Top Model: Westbank Wins the Woodward's War." *Terminal City Weekly*. Vancouver, 16 July 2004: 2.

————. "The Woodward's Phoenix Rises." *Terminal City Weekly*. Vancouver. 14 October 2004: 5.

Weder, Adele. "It Makes a Village." *Azure* 22, NO.166 (March/April 2006): 94-98. About the Woodward's Redevelopment Project.

TELEVISION AND VIDEO

City of Vancouver, Greater Vancouver Regional District, and Shaw. *Woodward's Design Competition*. VANCOUVER: GVTV, 17 February 2005. VIDEO. 8 May 2006.
<http://vancouver.ca/greaterdot_wa/index.cfm?fuseaction=GVTV.storyDet&storyid=456>.

City of Vancouver, Greater Vancouver Regional District, and Shaw. *Woodward's Developer/Architect Profile*. VANCOUVER: GVTV, 3 March 2005. VIDEO. 8 May 2006.
<http://vancouver.ca/Greaterdot_wa/index.cfm?fuseaction=GVTV.storyDet&storyid=458>.

Duncan, Robert and Carolyn Schmidt. *Woodward's: the Competition*. VANCOUVER: INTERNATIONAL DOCUMENTARY TELEVISION CORPORATION IN ASSOCIATION WITH CBC NEWSWORLD and with support from CBC BRITISH COLUMBIA, 2005.

PROFESSIONAL AWARDS AND COMPETITIONS

2004   **Winner of the Woodward's Competition**, Vancouver, B.C. with Westbank Projects/Peterson Investment Group as developer and Portland Hotel Society as community partner

2004   **Governor General's Medal in Architecture** for Lore Krill Housing Co-op and City of Vancouver Parkade

2004   Elected to the **Royal Canadian Academy of Arts**

2003   **BC Lieutenant Governor's Award in Architecture** for Lore Krill Housing Co-op and City of Vancouver Parkade

2001   **BC Lieutenant Governor's Medal in Architecture** for Coal Harbour Community Centre

2000   **BC Lieutenant Governor's Medal in Architecture** for Bruce Eriksen Place

Photograph credits

All photographs by **Christopher Grabowski** except as follows:

Stan Douglas – Front cover photo

Gregory Henriquez – Back cover collage of FIREHALL TRAINING TOWER; BELLA BELLA COMMUNITY SCHOOL 52

Peter Timmermans – FIREHALL TRAINING TOWER 18; ARTS UMBRELLA 28

Derek Lepper – BRUCE ERIKSEN PLACE 78; COAL HARBOUR COMMUNITY CENTRE 90; LORE KRILL HOUSING CO-OP 6, 128

Robert Duncan and Carolyn Schmidt – stills from video *Woodward's: the Competition* of Jim Green 116; stills from video *Woodward's: the Competition* of Gregory Henriquez and Ian Gillespie, President of Westbank Projects Corporation 160

Colin Goldie – WOODWARD'S REDEVELOPMENT model 162

First published in 2006 by BLUE*IM*PRINT

Library and Archives Canada Cataloguing in Publication

 Towards an Ethical Architecture: Issues within the work of Gregory Henriquez/essays by Alberto Perez-Gomez ... [et al.].

ISBN-10: 1-894965-50-7
ISBN-13: 978-1-894965-50-7

 1. Henriquez, Gregory. 2. Architects--Professional ethics.
3. Architecture--Moral and ethical aspects. I. Pérez-Gómez, Alberto, 1949-

NA749.H445P47 2006   174'.972092   C2006-903696-9

Printed and bound in China by Colorprint Offset

We gratefully acknowledge the support of the Canada Council for the Arts for our publishing program.

**Canada Council   Conseil des Arts
for the Arts   du Canada**

BOOK DESIGN BY **Elisa Gutiérrez**